THIS BOOK BELONGS TO:

Test Your Colors Here

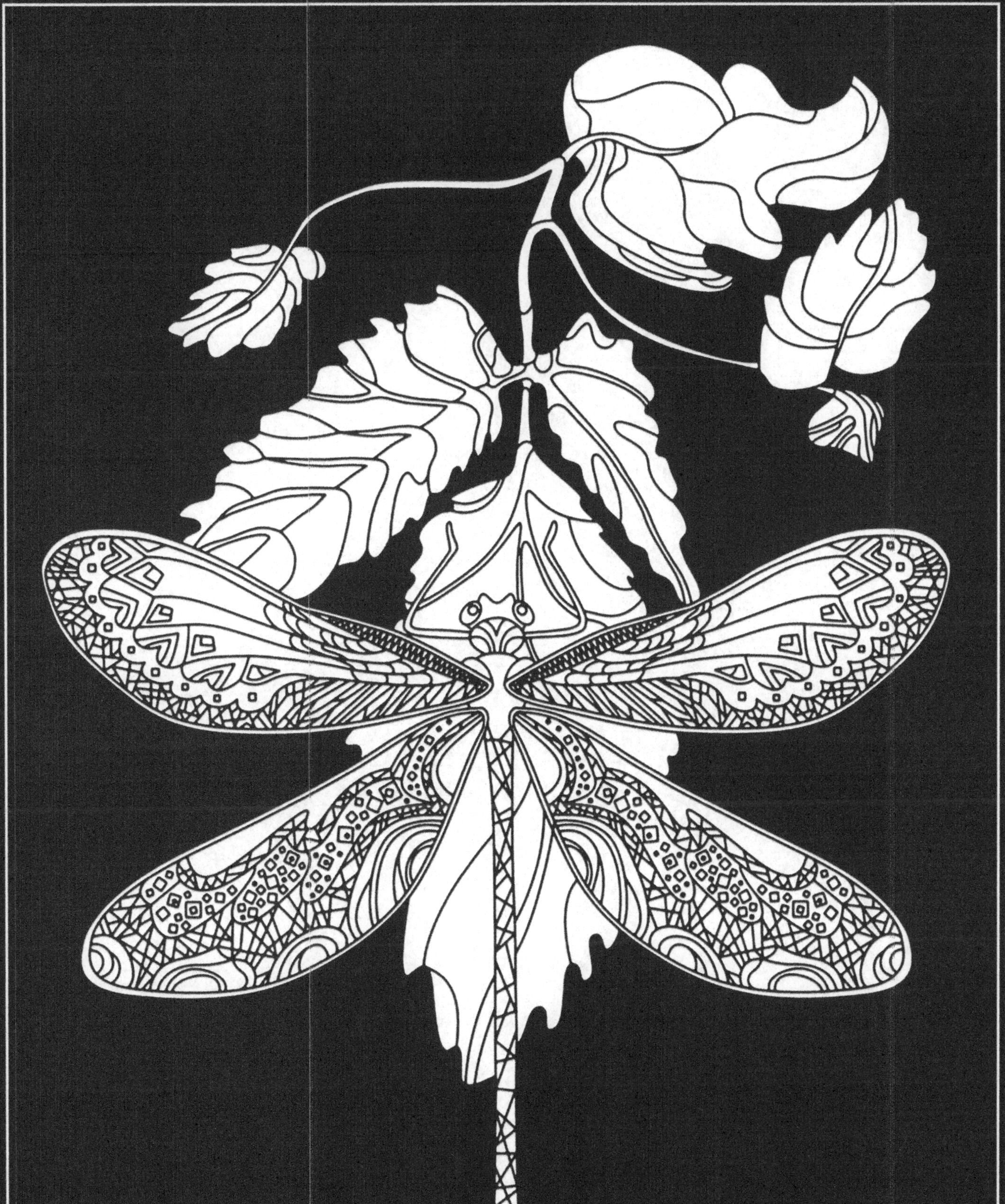

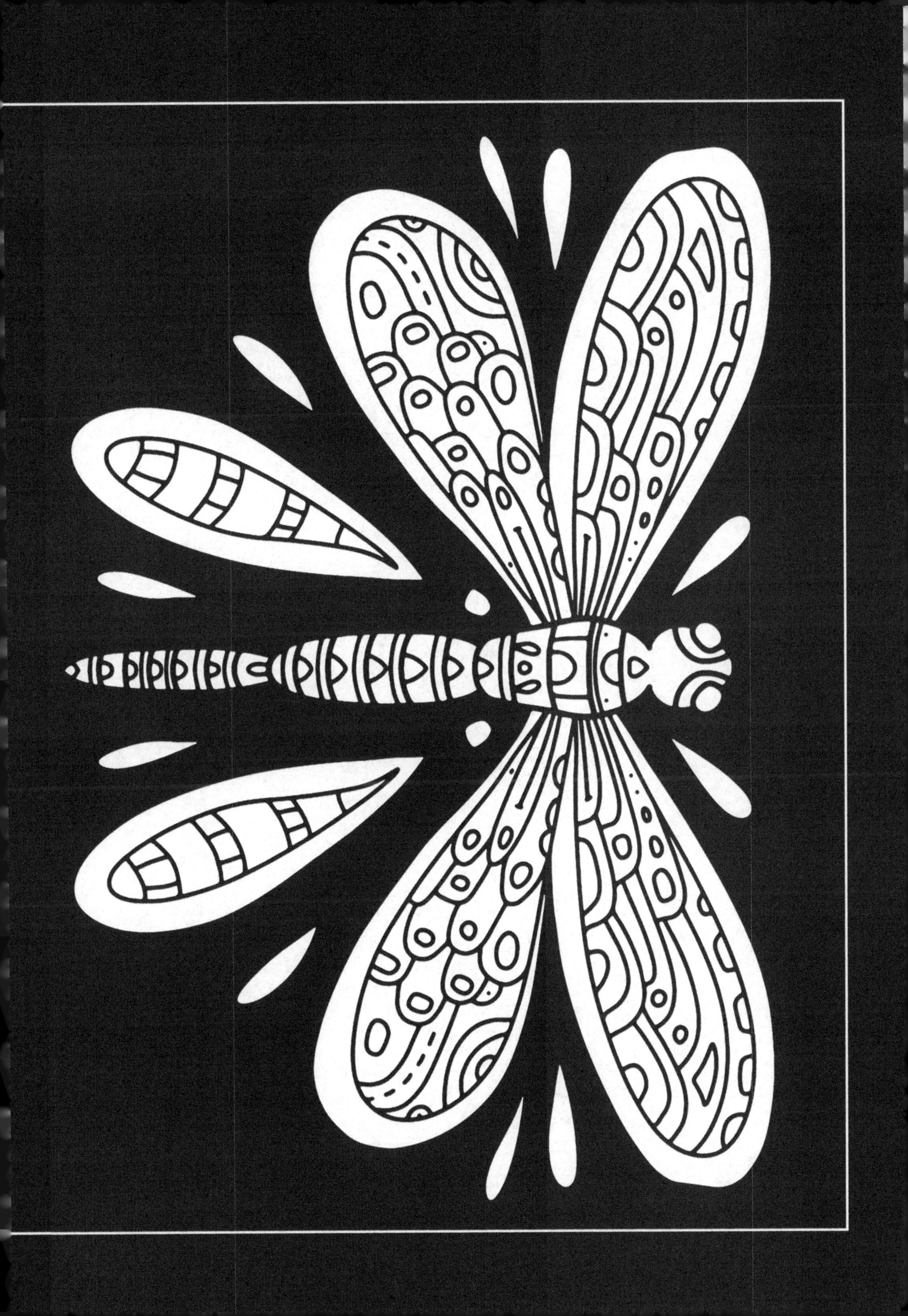

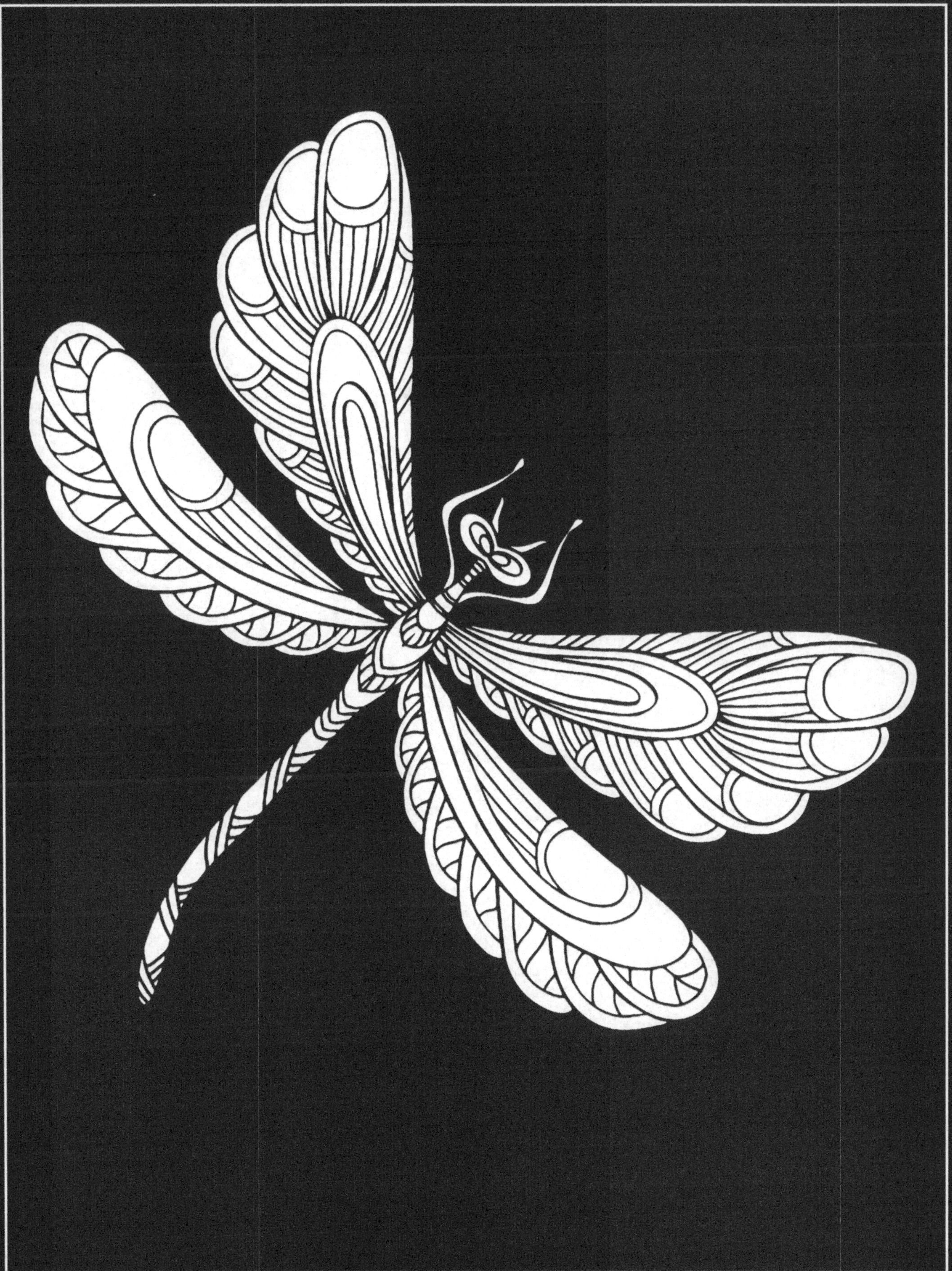

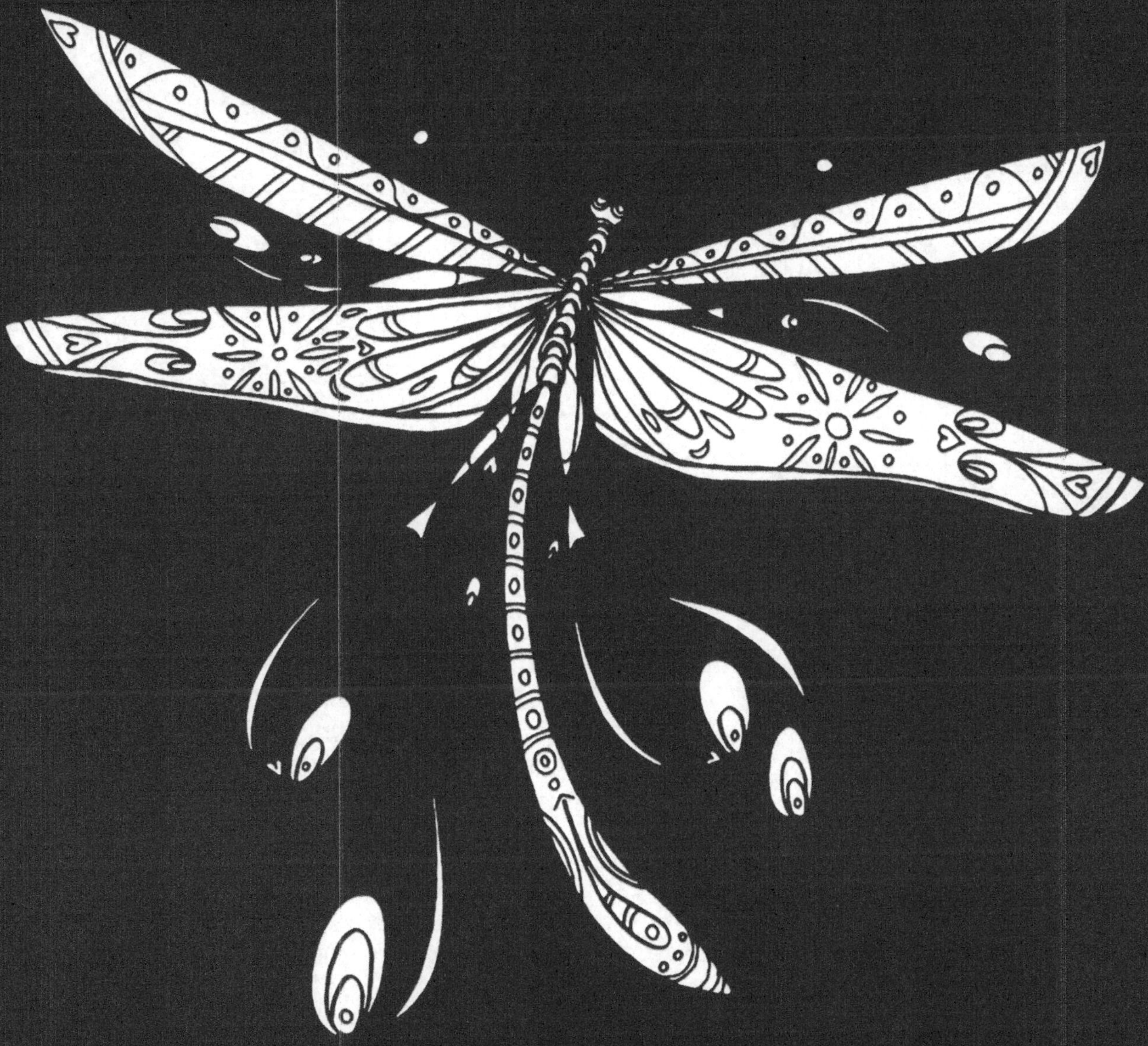

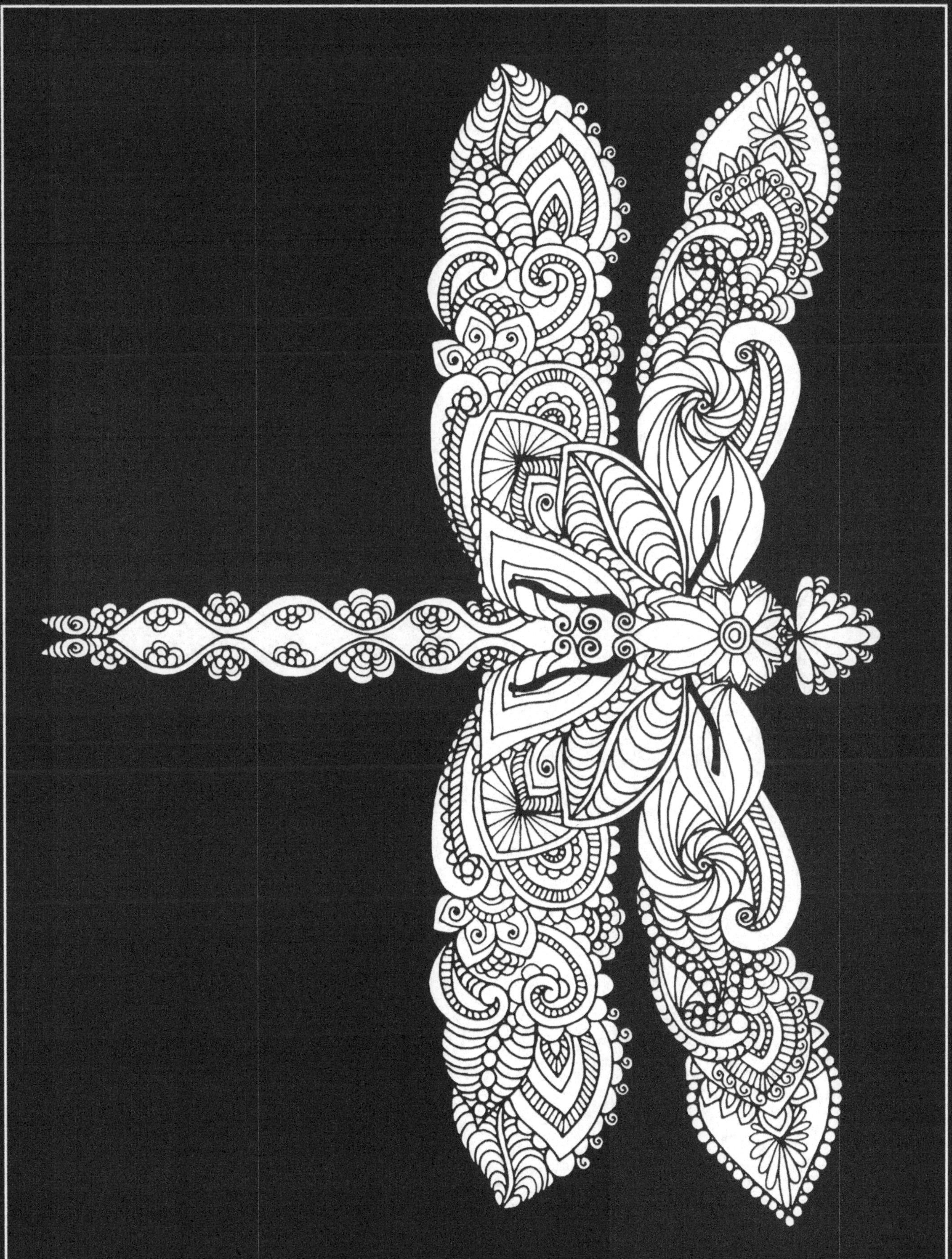

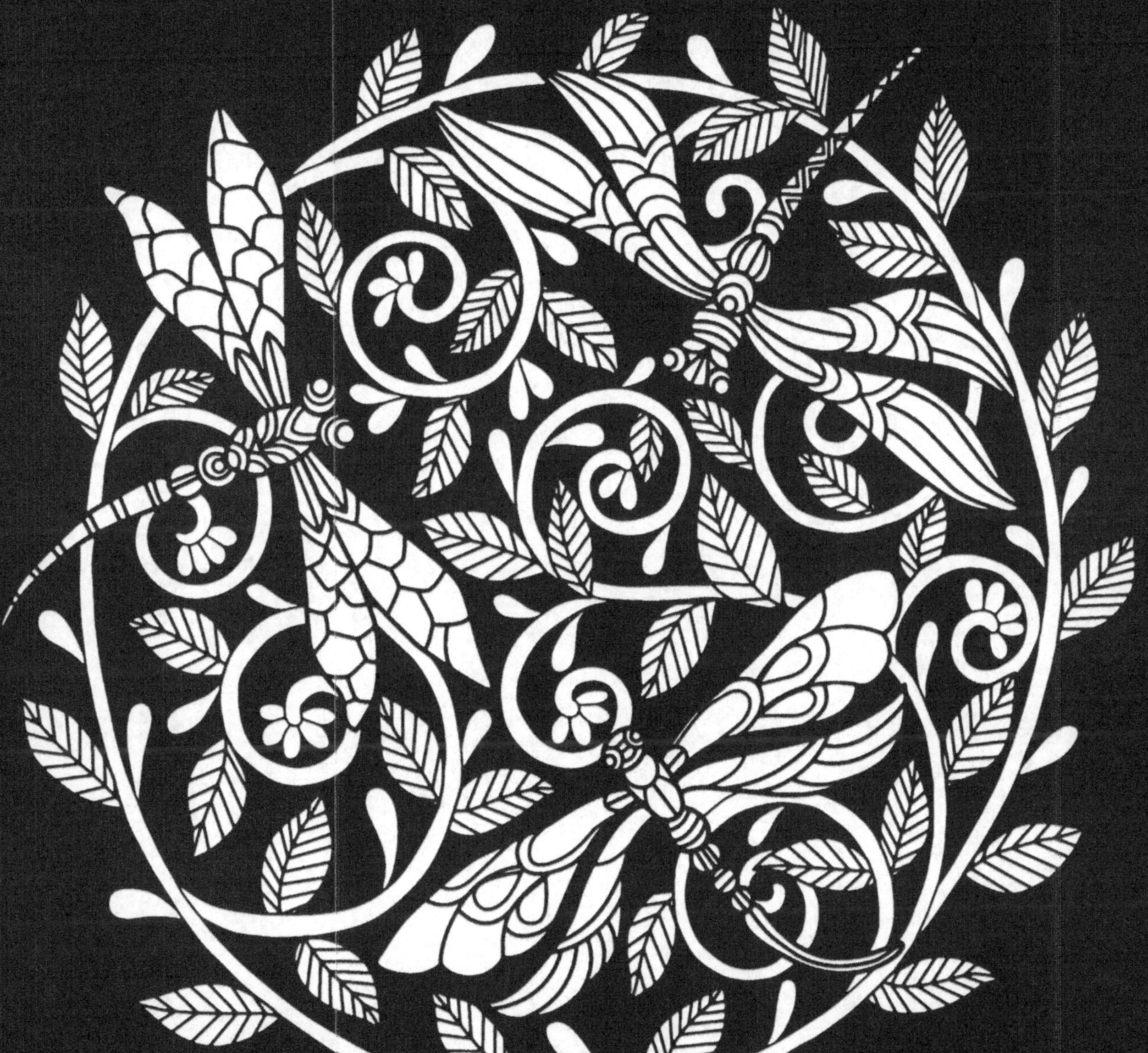

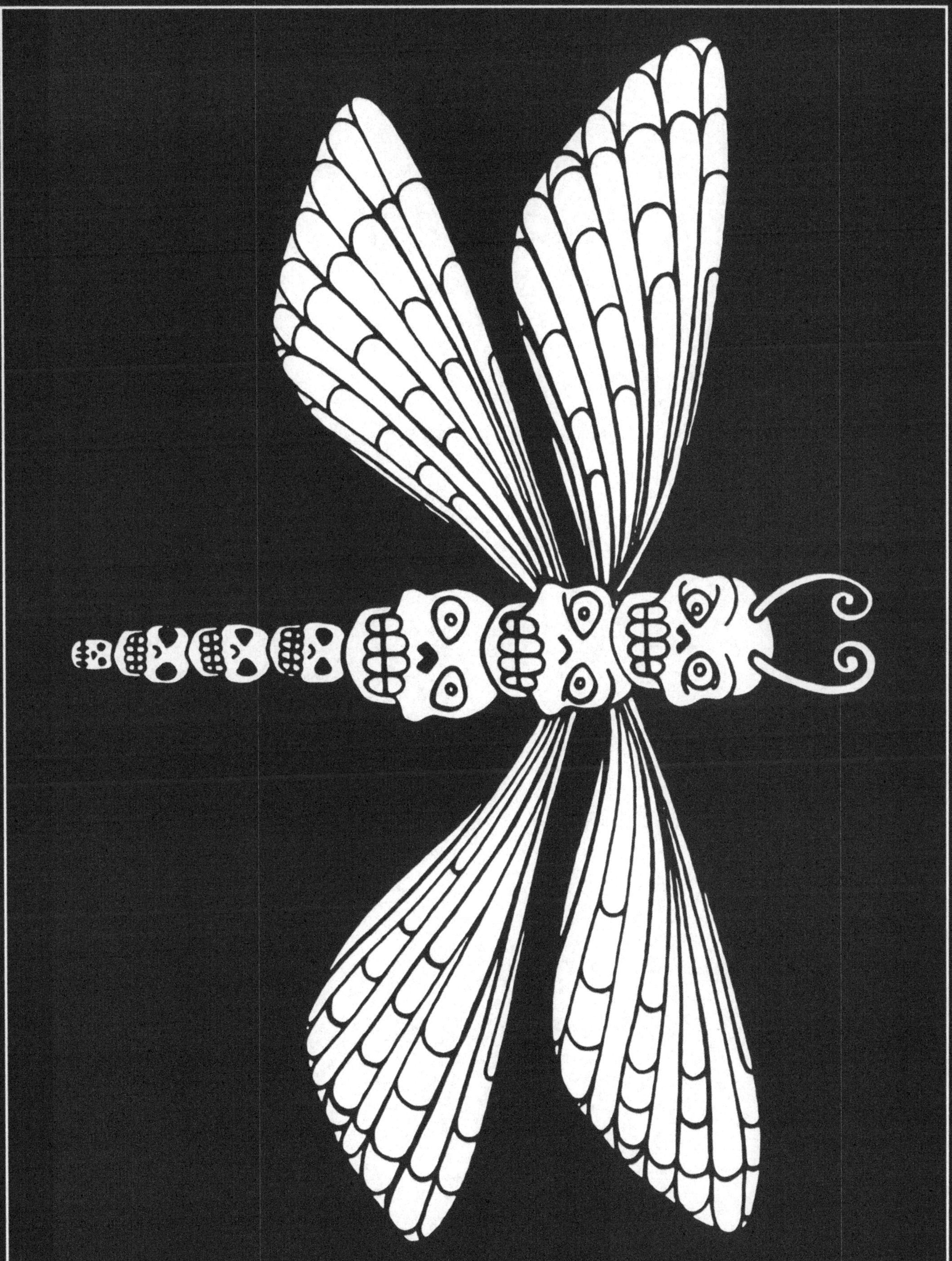

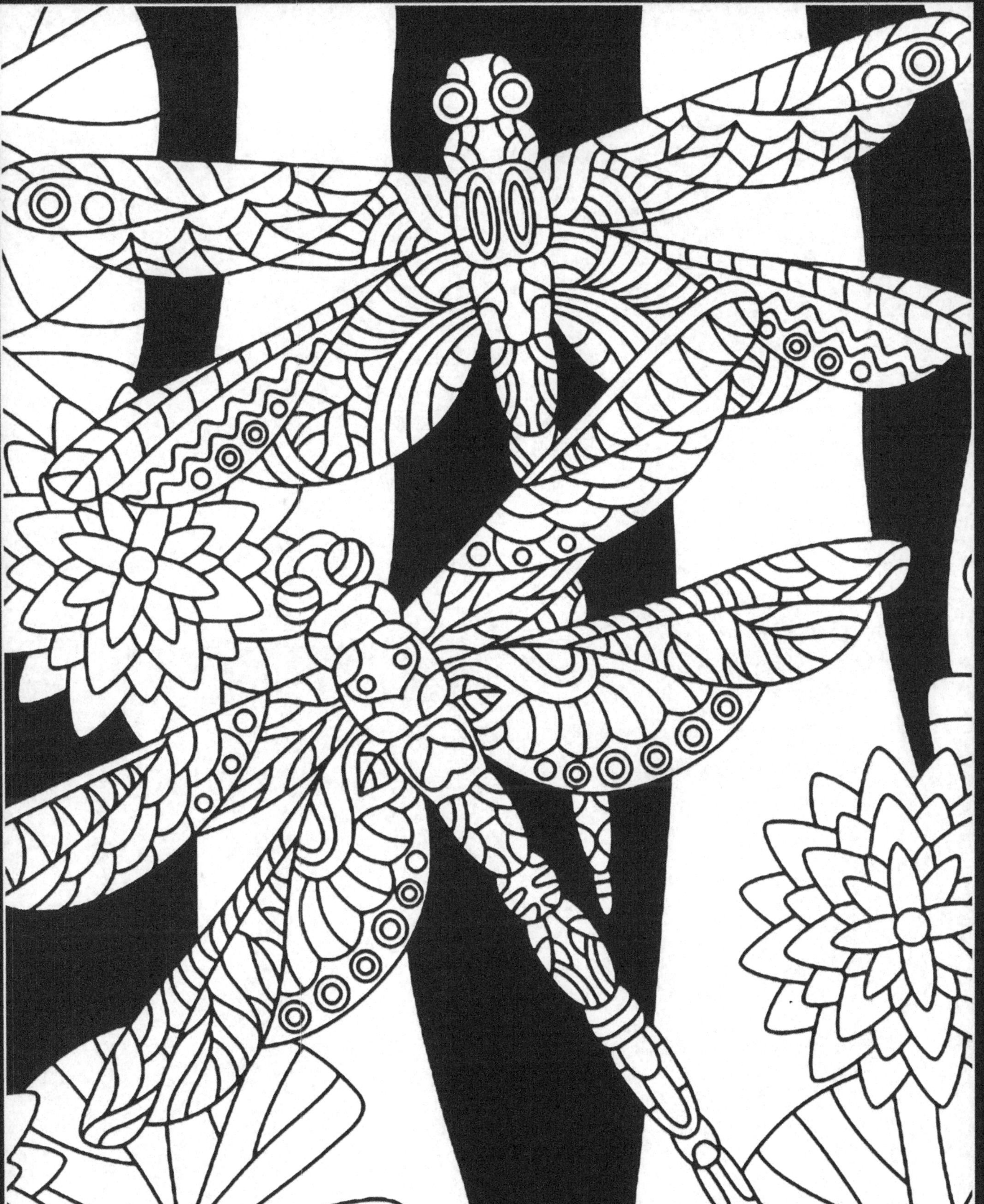

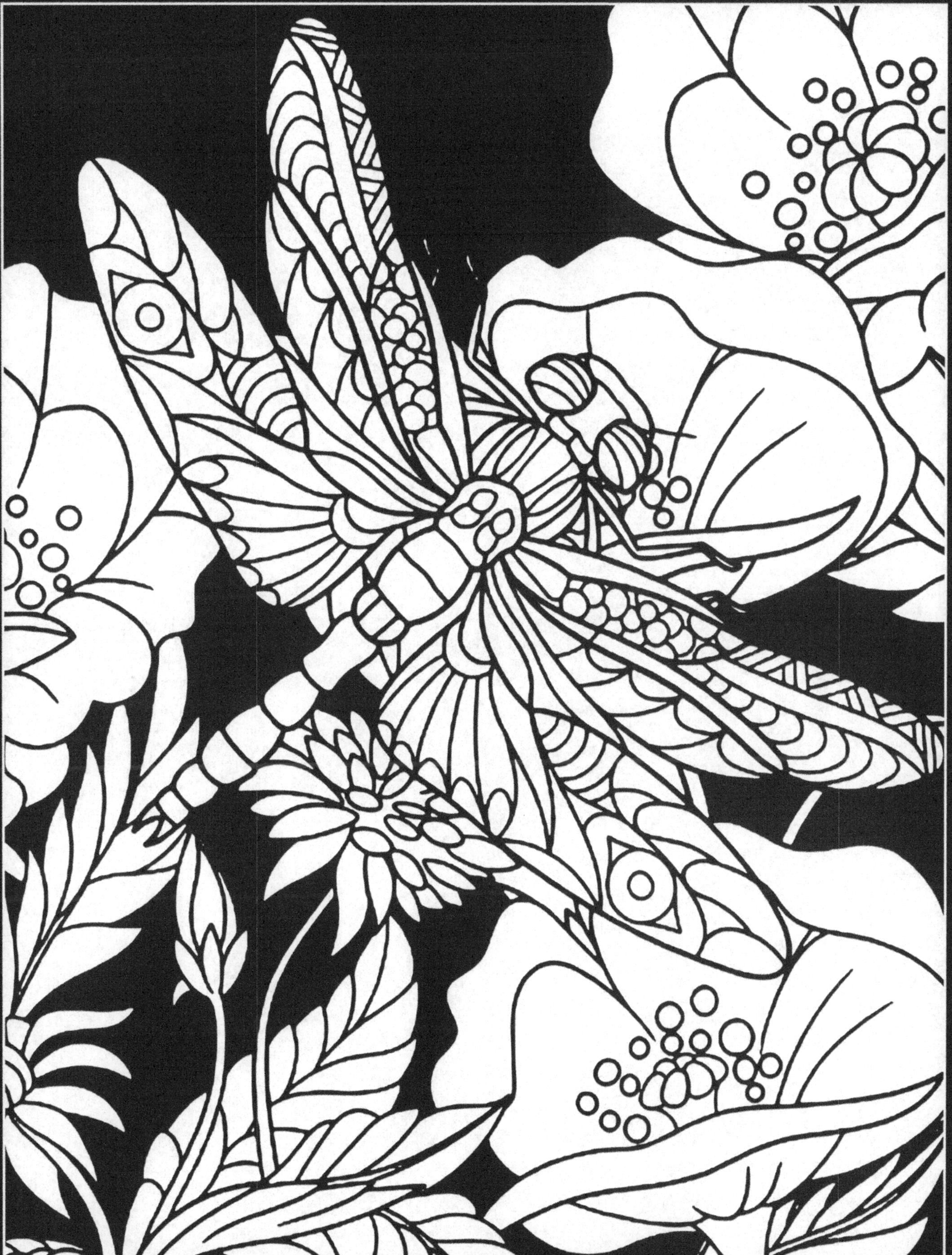

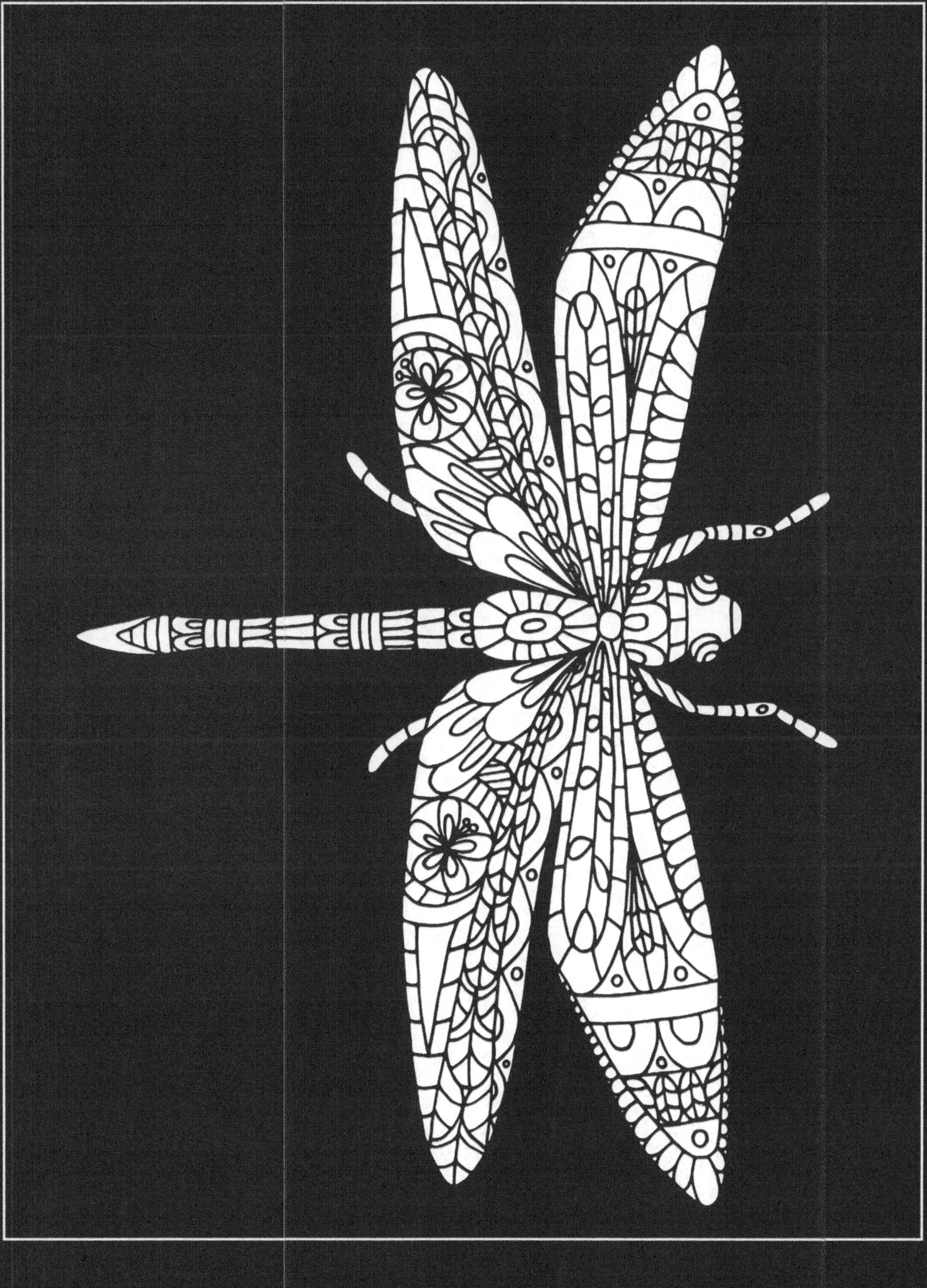

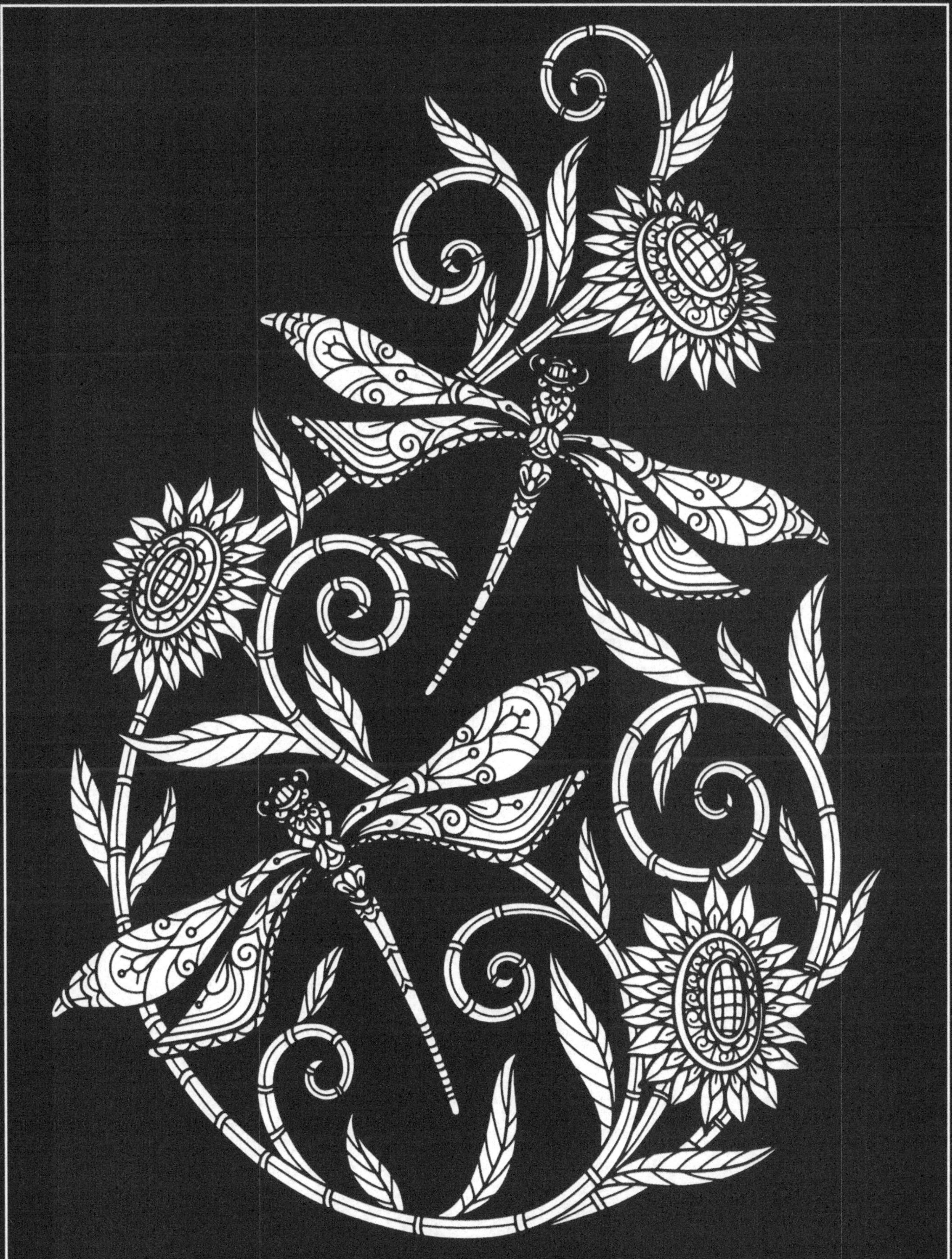

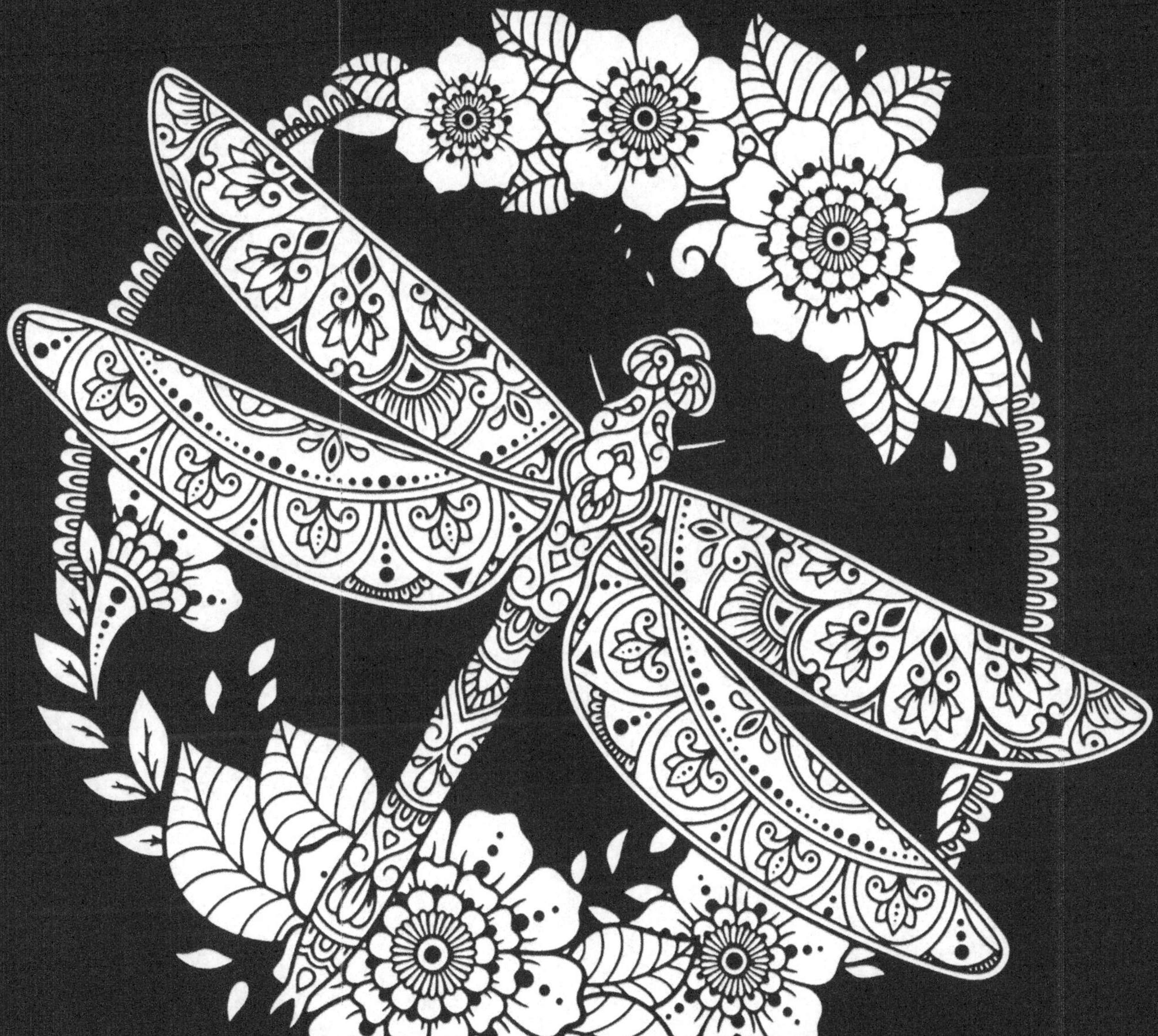

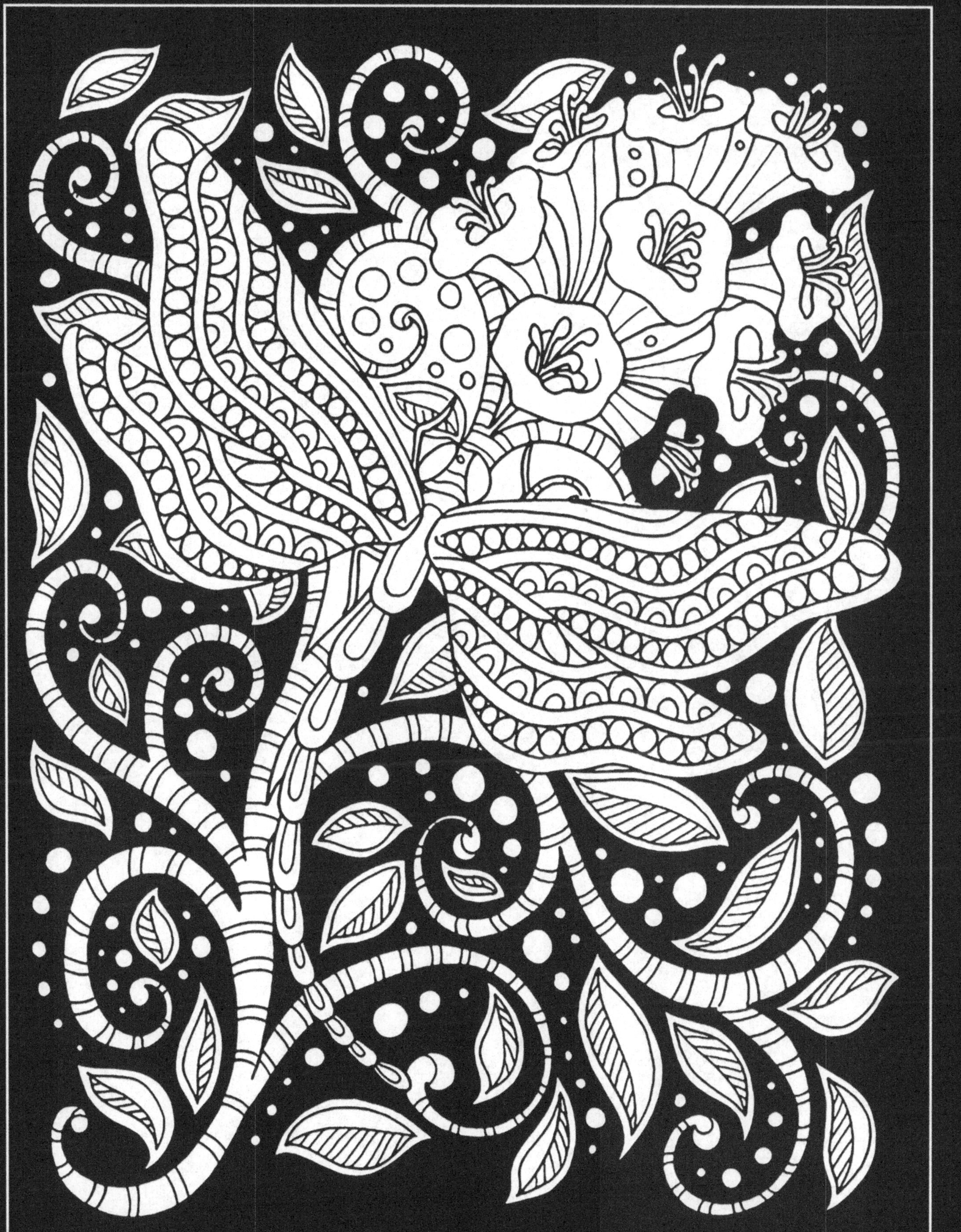

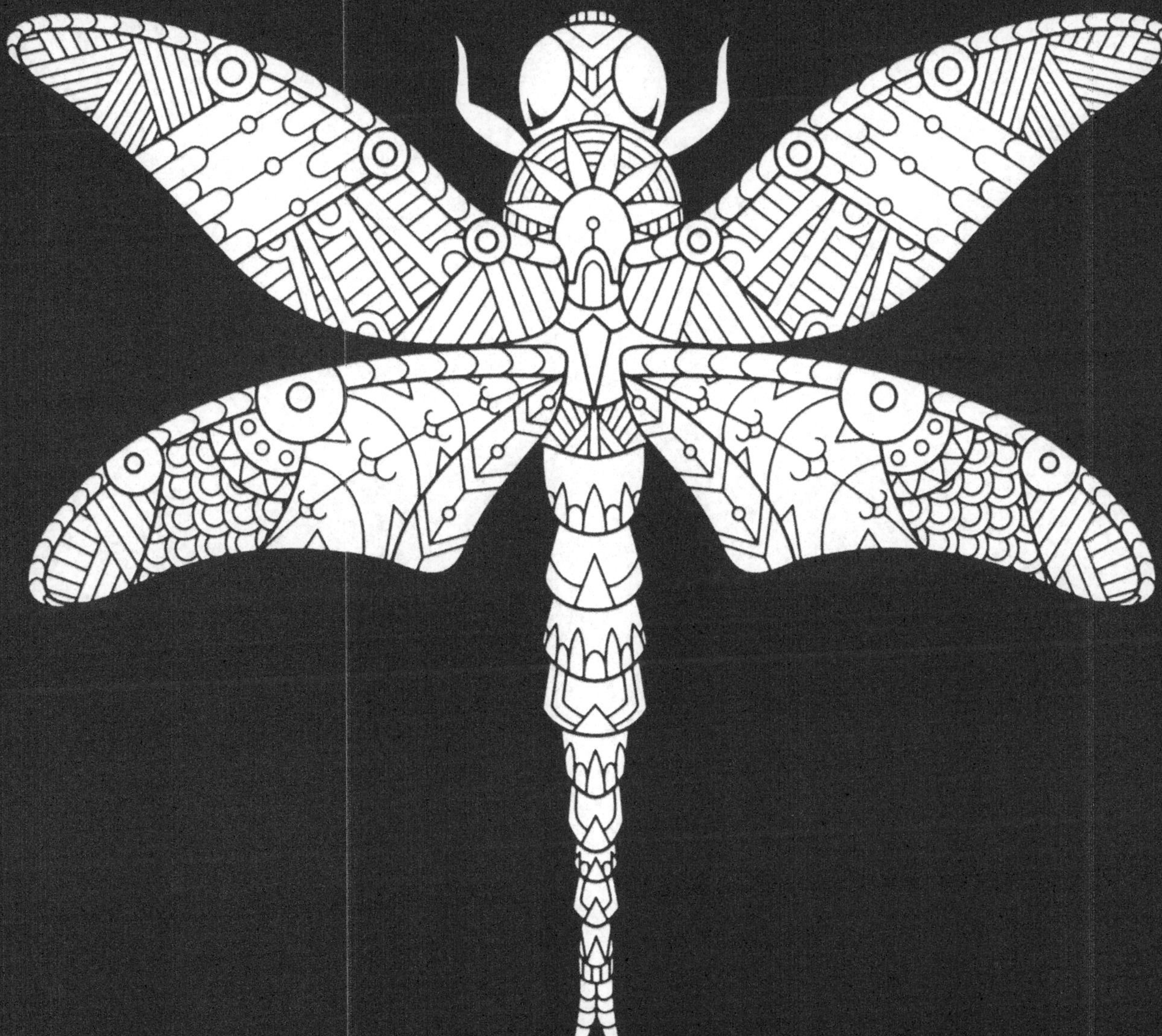

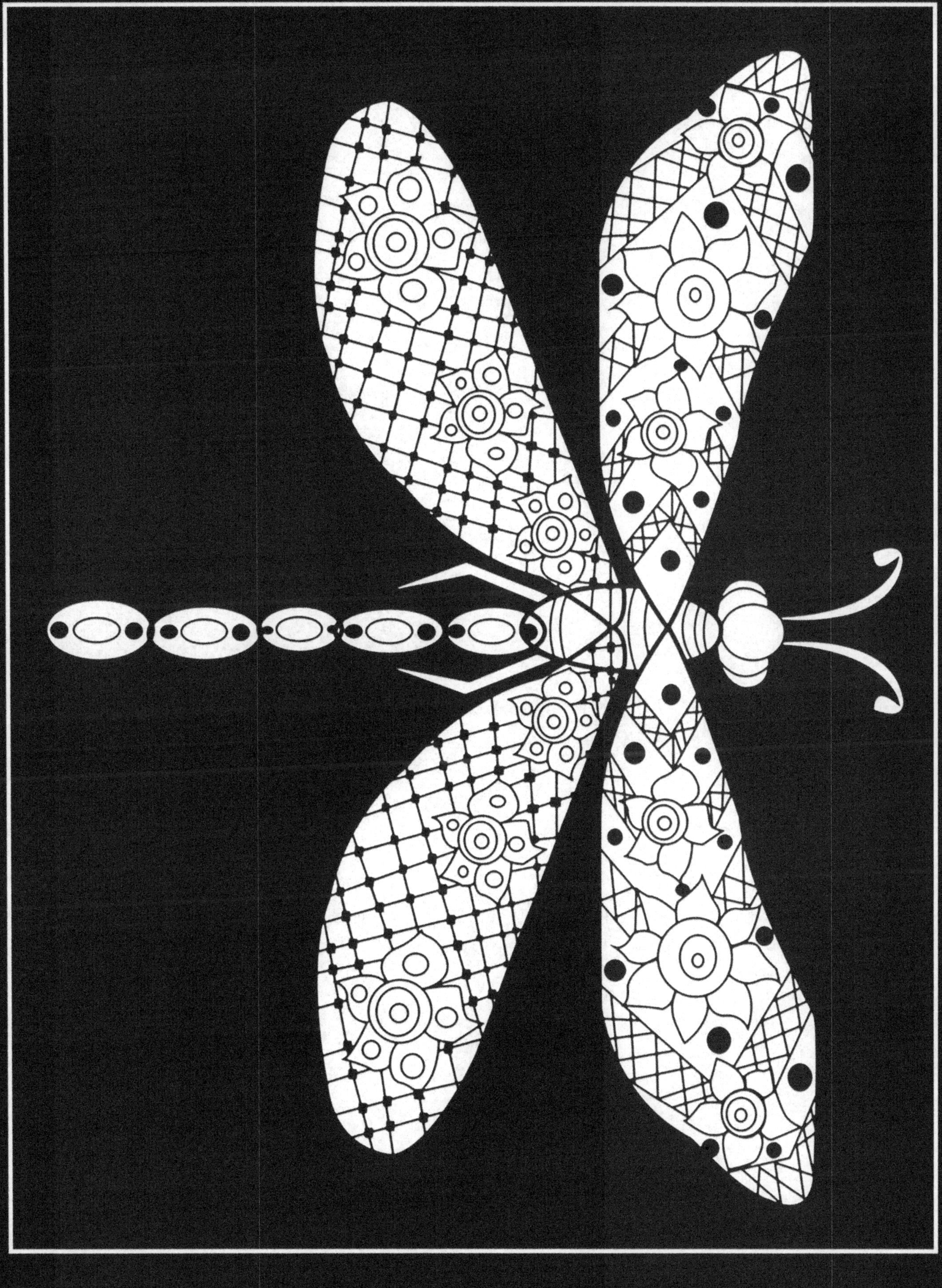

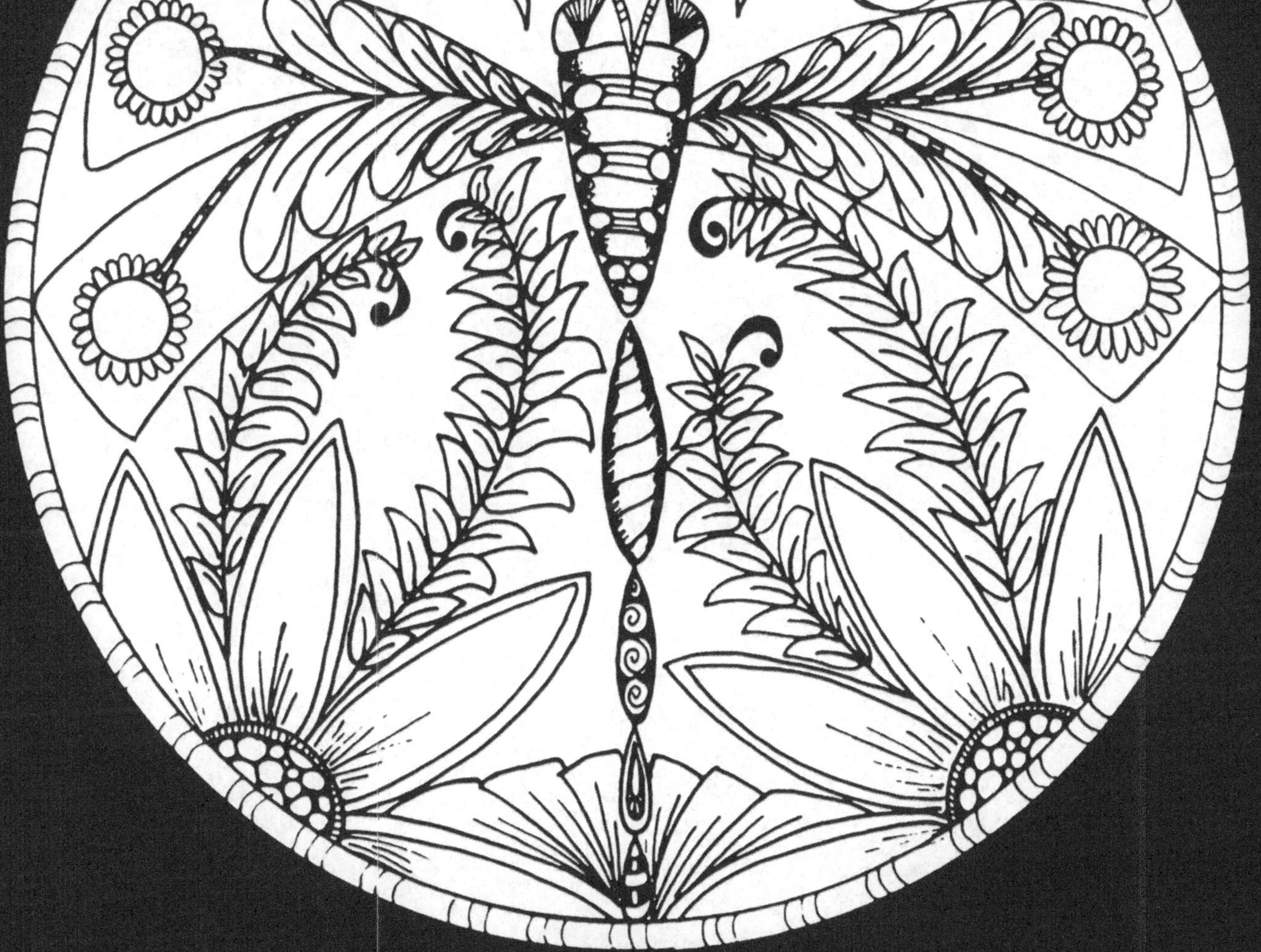

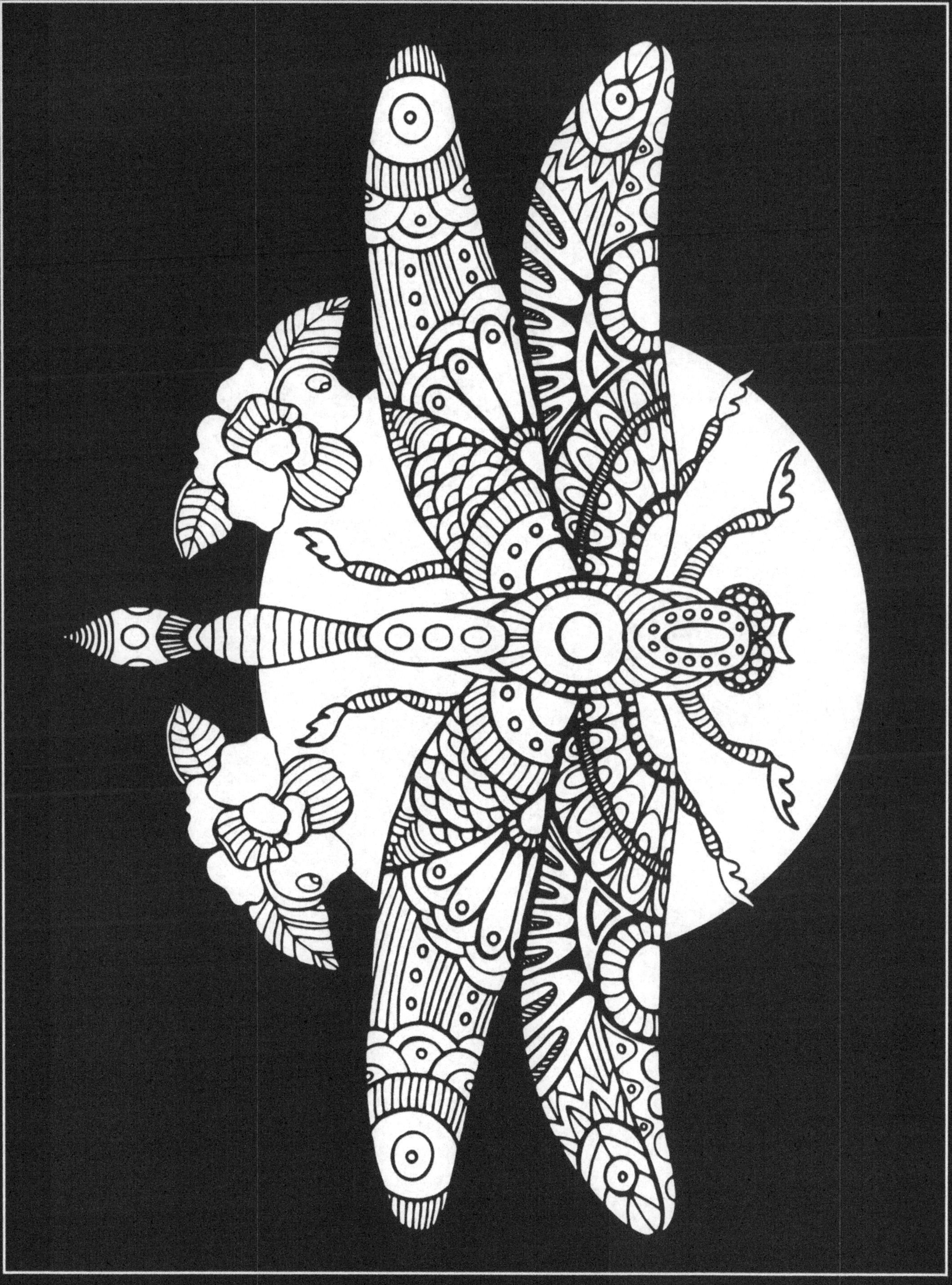

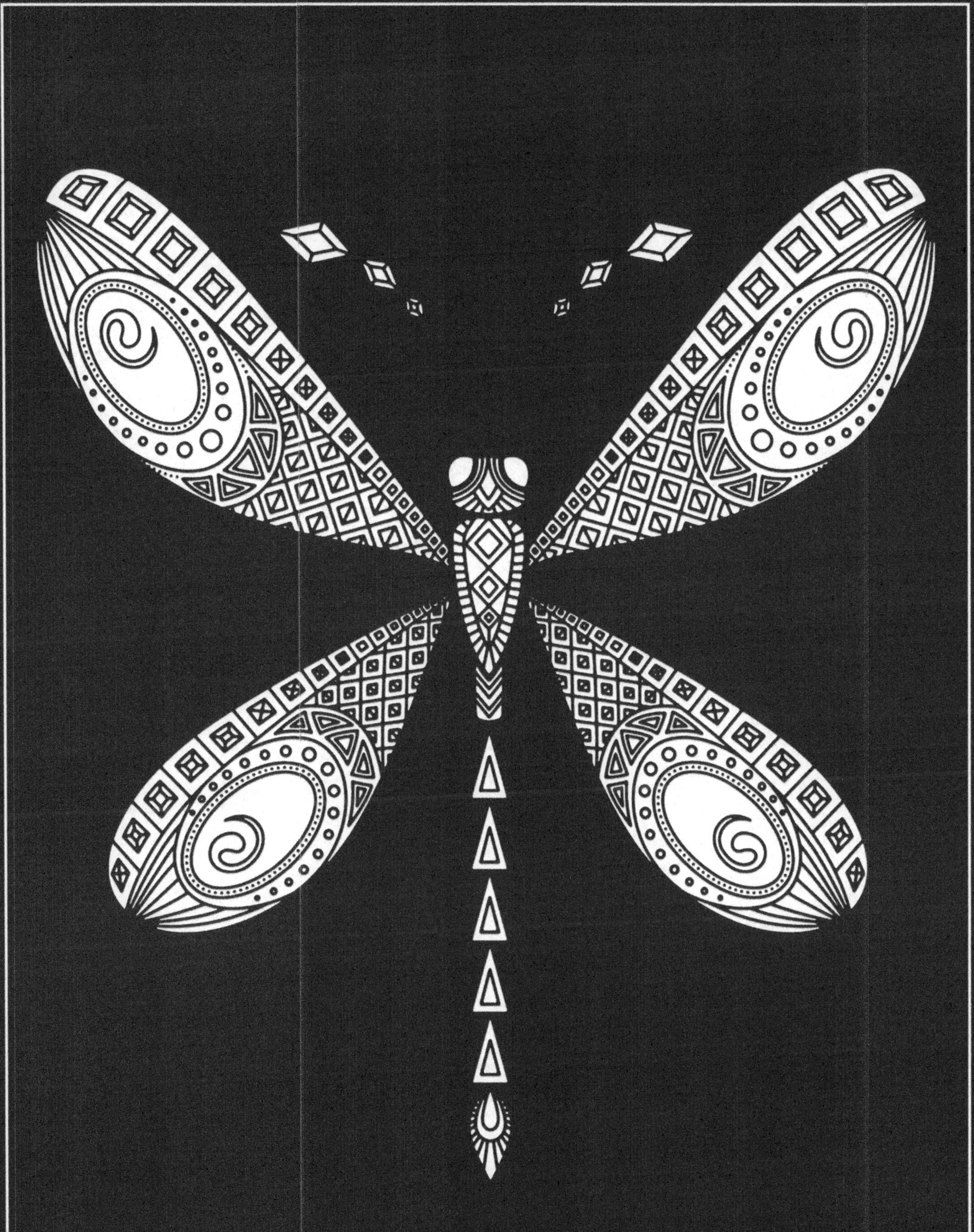

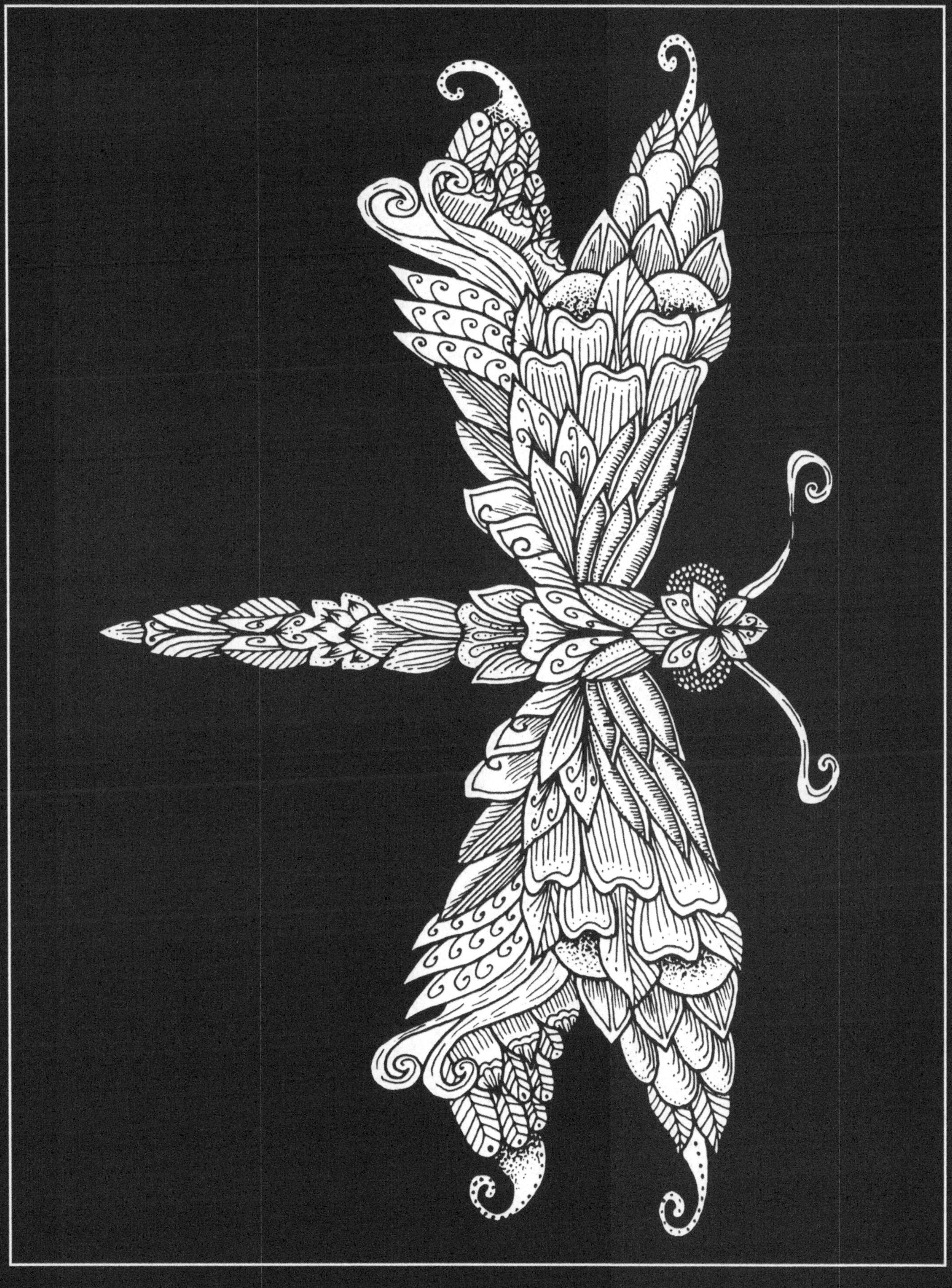

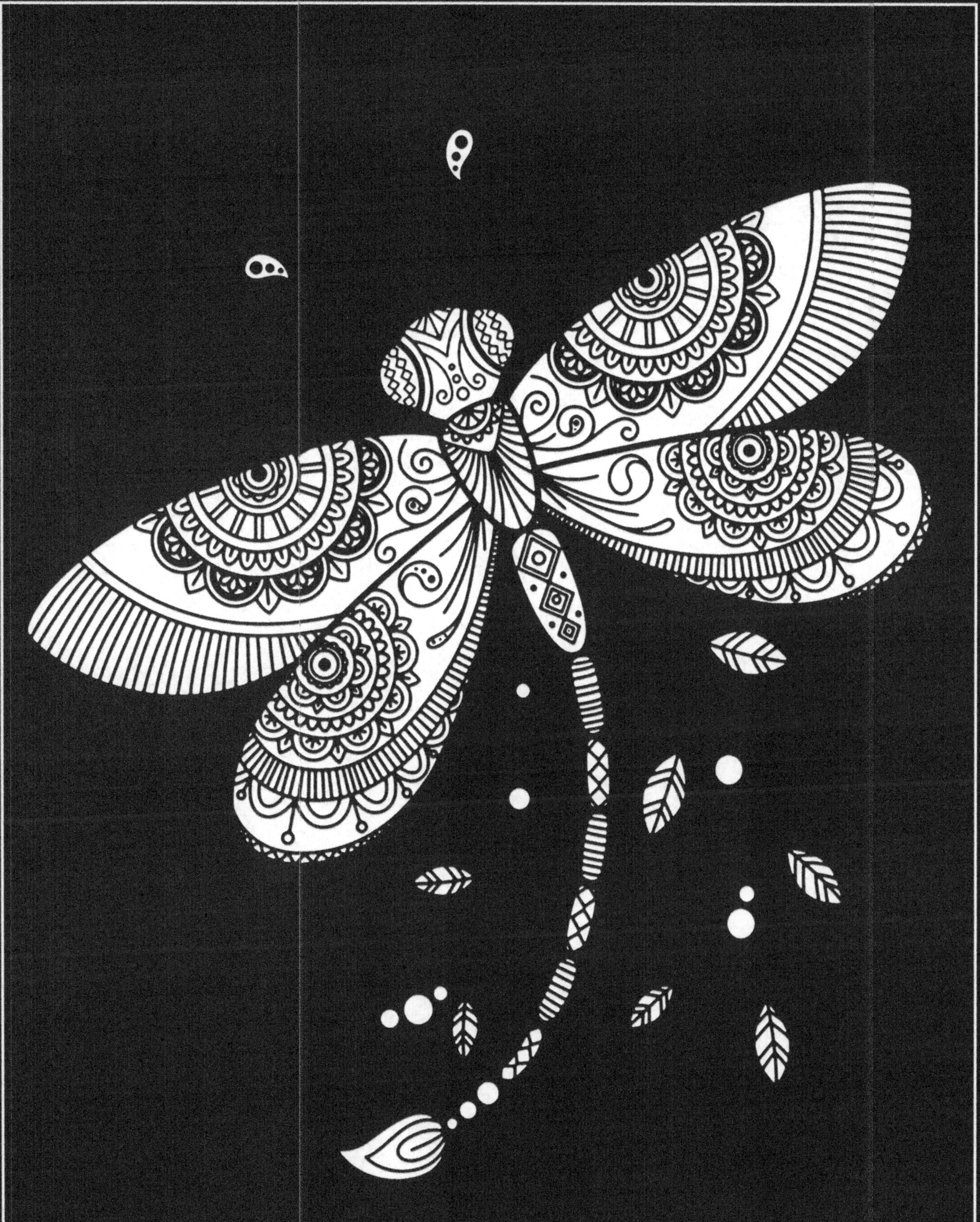

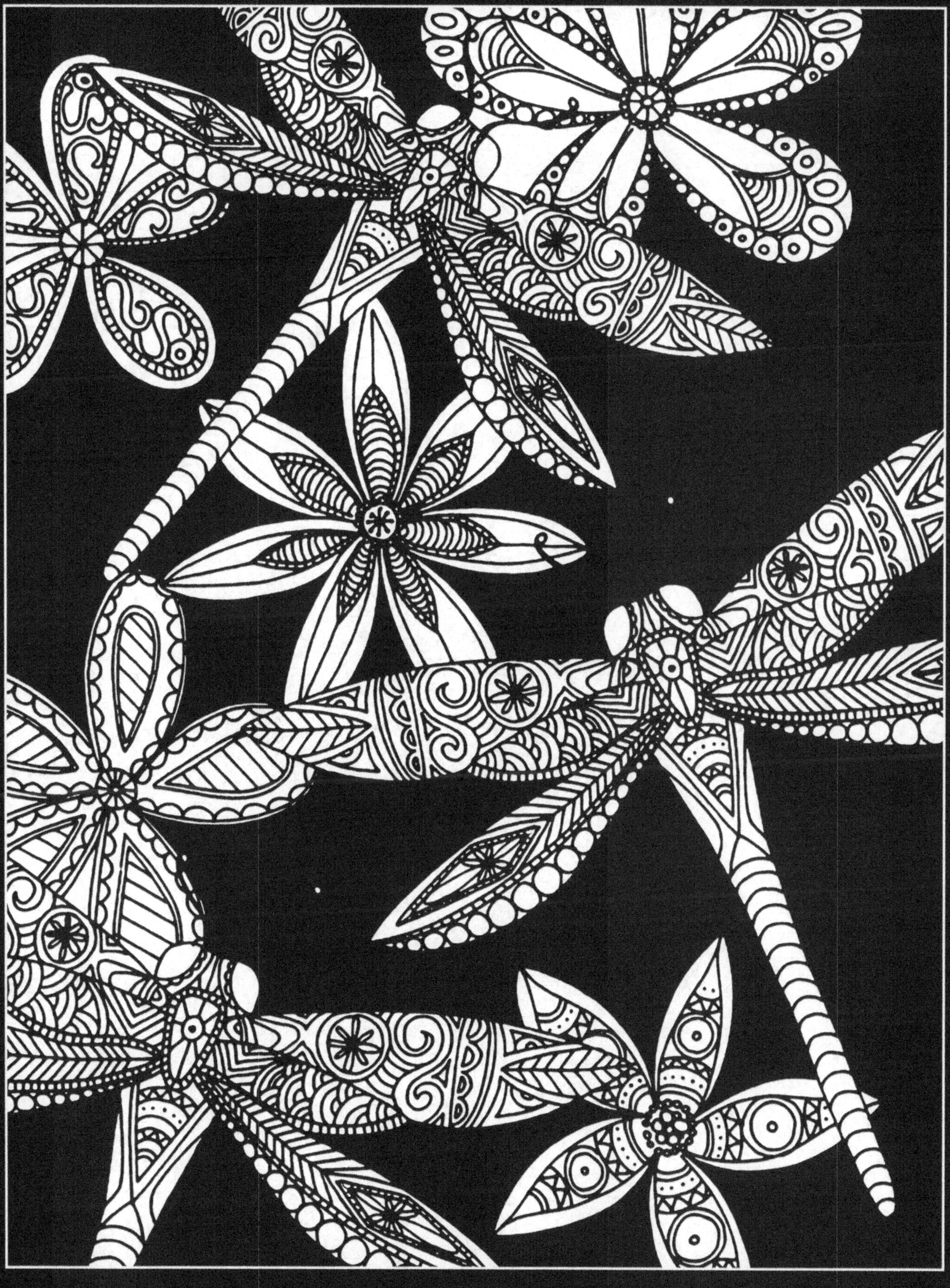

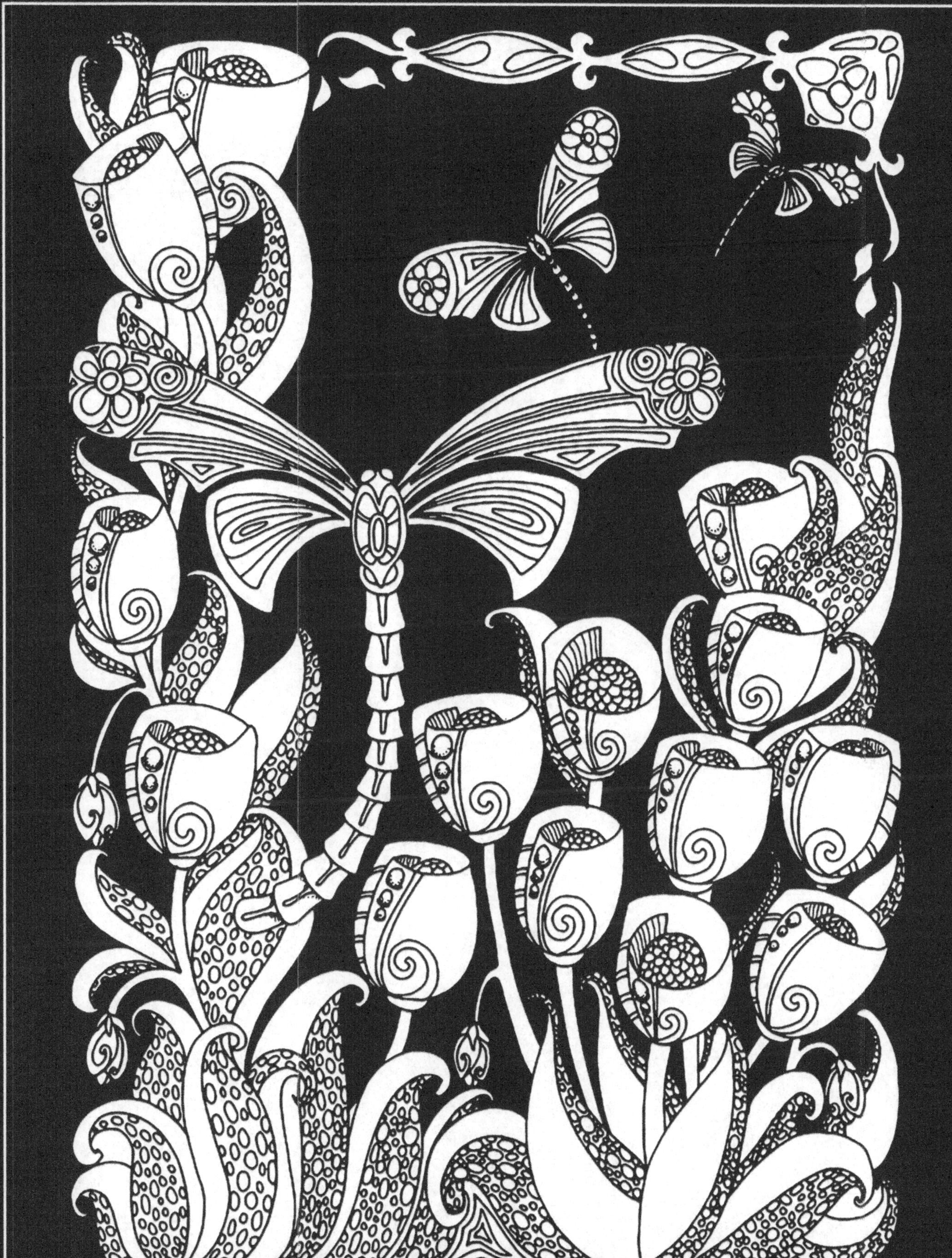

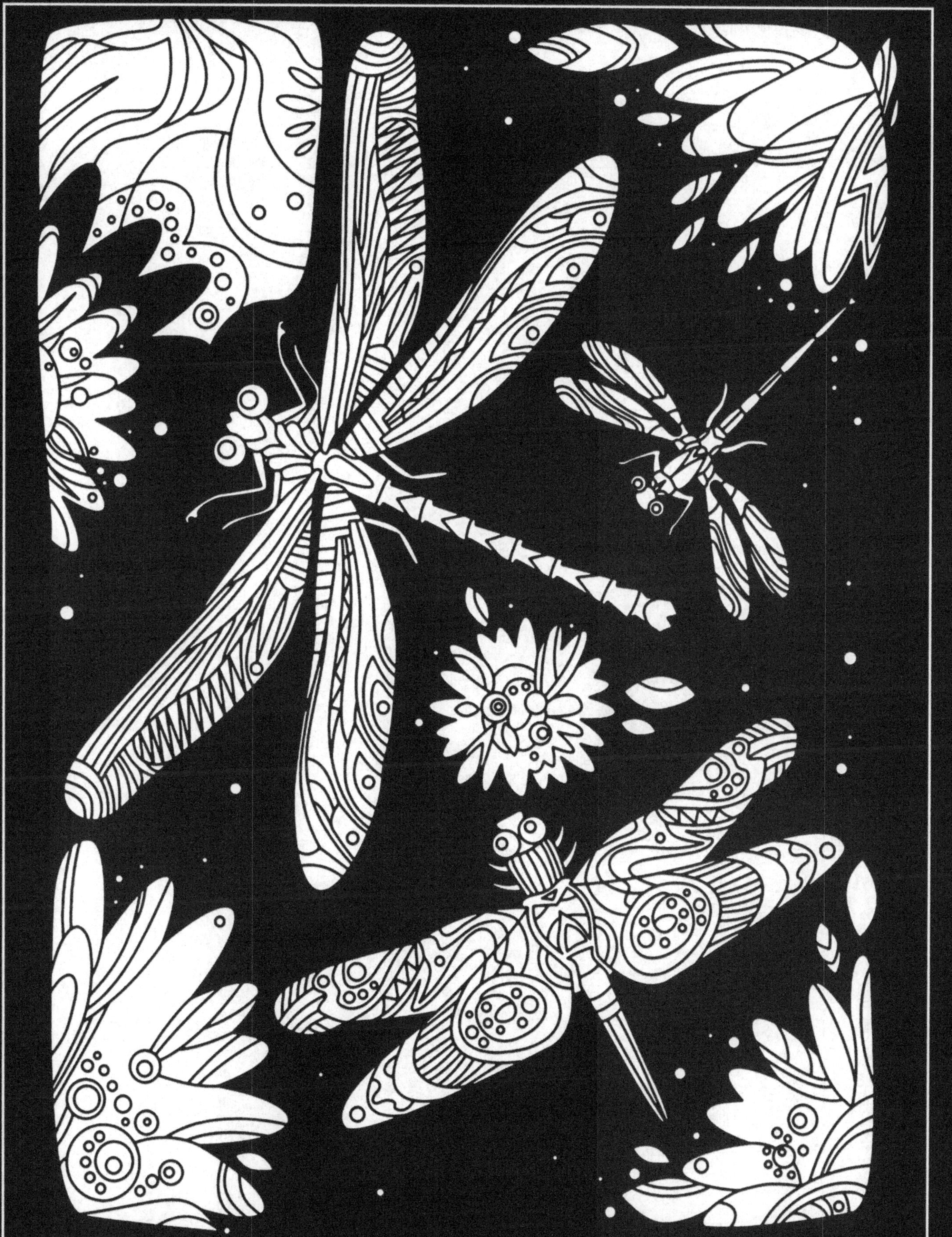

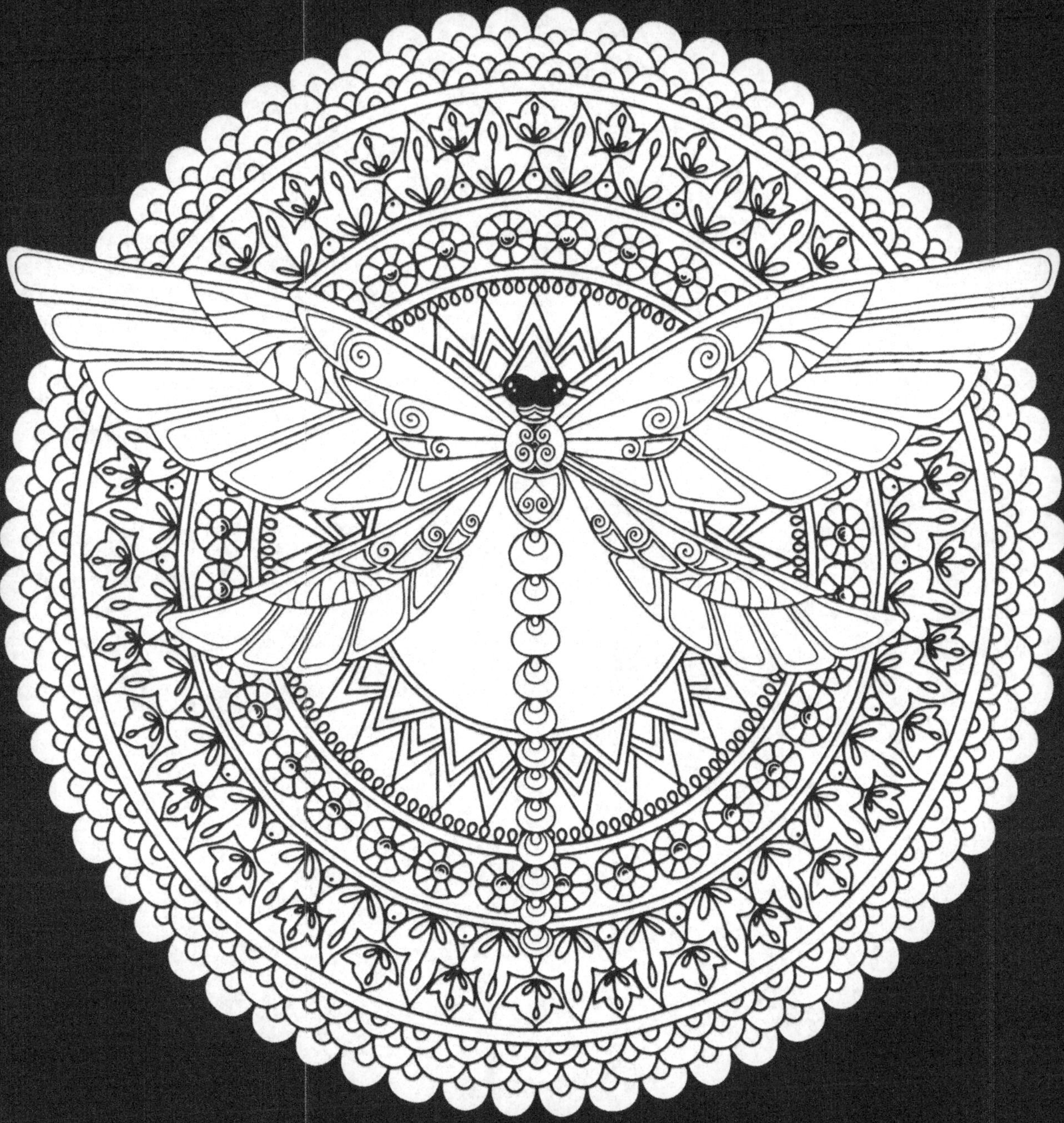

Made in the USA
Las Vegas, NV
13 March 2023

69002187R00031